Library of Congress Cataloging-in-Publication Data

Back, Christine.
    Spider's web.

    (Stopwatch books)
    Includes index.
    Summary: Text and photographs describe how a garden
spider spins her web and how she uses it to catch food.
    1. Spider webs—Juvenile literature. 2. Spiders—
Juvenile literature. [1. Spider webs. 2. Spiders]
I. Watts, Barrie, ill. II. Title. III. Series.
QL458.4.B33 1986   595.4'40453   86-10017
ISBN 0-382-09303-8
ISBN 0-382-09288-0 (lib. bdg.)

First published by A&C Black (Publishers) Limited
35 Bedford Row, London WC1R 4JH

© 1984 A&C Black (Publishers) Limited

Published in the United States in 1986
by Silver Burdett Press,
Englewood Cliffs, New Jersey

Acknowledgements
The artwork is by B L Kearley Ltd.

Spider's web

Christine Back
Photographs by Barrie Watts

Stopwatch books

Silver Burdett Press • Englewood Cliffs, New Jersey

The spider is going to make a web.

This book tells you how a garden spider spins its web.

Here is a female spider starting her web. First she spins a thread. The spider sticks one end of the thread to a twig. She lets the other end flutter in the wind. Soon this end sticks onto a leaf.

Now the thread is stretched between a twig and a leaf. It looks like this.

Look at the photograph. The thread is very thin, so you cannot see all of it. But it is very strong.

The thread comes out of the spider's body.

Look at this photograph.

At the end of the spider's body, there are six tiny tubes.
Can you see them? The tubes are called spinnerets.
The thread comes out of the spinnerets.

Look at the big photograph. You can see the spider
pulling a thread out of her body. The spider uses
two legs to pull out the thread. She holds onto the
web with her other legs.

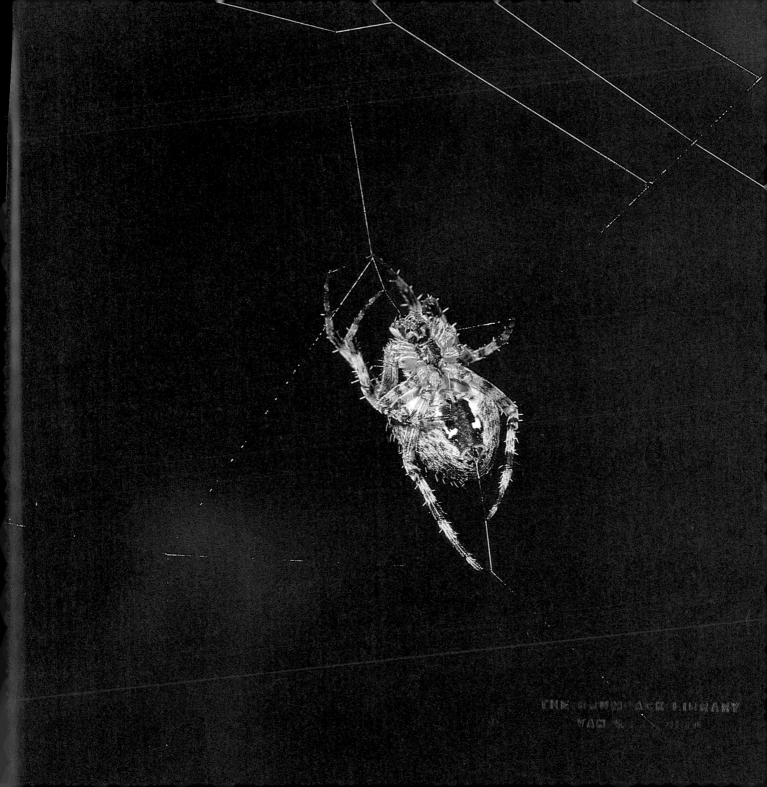

The spider makes a frame for her web.

The spider spins some more threads. She fastens each
thread to a twig or leaf. These threads will be
the outside of the web.

Next, the spider spins some threads that look like
the spokes of a wheel.
Now the web looks like this.

Look at the photograph. Can you see two threads that
look like the spokes of a wheel?

The spider makes the web stronger.

In the middle of the web, the spider spins a spiral of thread.
Now the web looks like this.

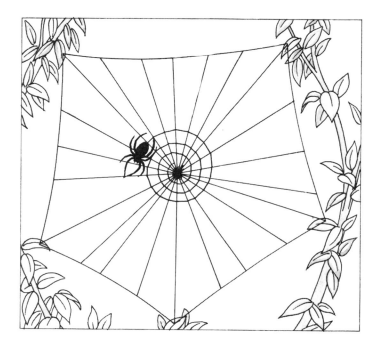

Look at the photograph. Can you see the spiral of
thread in the middle of the web?

The spider spins special sticky threads.

The spider starts to spin new threads. She goes around the edge of the web, like this.

The new part of the web is made from special sticky threads.

Look at the photograph. Can you see the blobs of sticky stuff on the threads? What do you think they are for?

The spider keeps spinning more sticky threads.

The spider gets nearer and nearer to the middle of the web.

Look at this drawing.

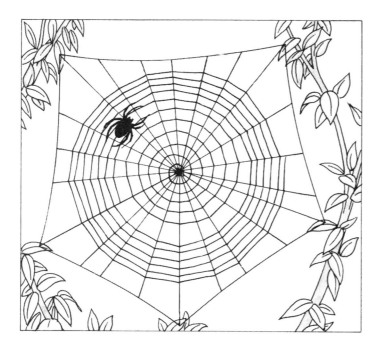

When the spider gets near the middle of the web,
she eats the spiral of thread that she made there
before. This makes room for more sticky threads.

Look at the photograph. Can you see the spider in the
middle of the web? She is eating the threads there.

The spider's web is finished.

Look at the drawing.

You can see all the threads in the web.

Now look at the photograph. The sticky threads show up best.

A web this shape is called an orb web. Spider's webs are not all the same shape as this one. Different kinds of spiders make different shaped webs.

The spider waits near the web.

The spider has made her web for catching food.
She will eat any insects that fly into the web.

The spider hides near the web. She keeps hold of a thin
thread that is joined to the web. If something flies
into the web, the spider will feel the thread move.

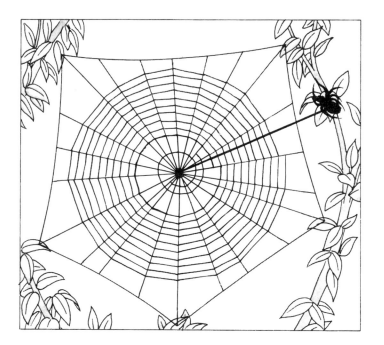

Look at the photograph. Can you see the spider
holding the thread?

An insect gets caught in the web.

The spider doesn't have to wait very long. An insect flies into the web and gets caught on the sticky threads. Look at the photograph. The insect is tearing the web as it tries to get away.

Now look at the drawing.

The spider feels the web move. She knows that there is food in the web.

The spider wraps the insect in thread.

The spider goes onto the web. She bites the
insect with her fangs. This puts poison into
the insect's body.

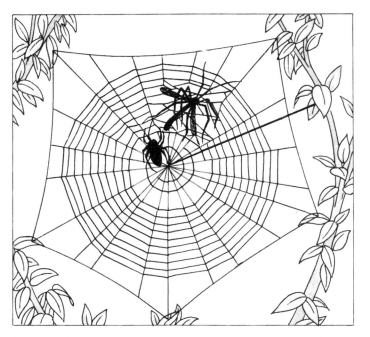

Now the insect stops struggling. It is
still alive but it cannot move. The spider
wraps the insect in silk thread.

Look at the photograph. Can you see the insect
inside the parcel of thread? It will stay there until
the spider is ready to eat.

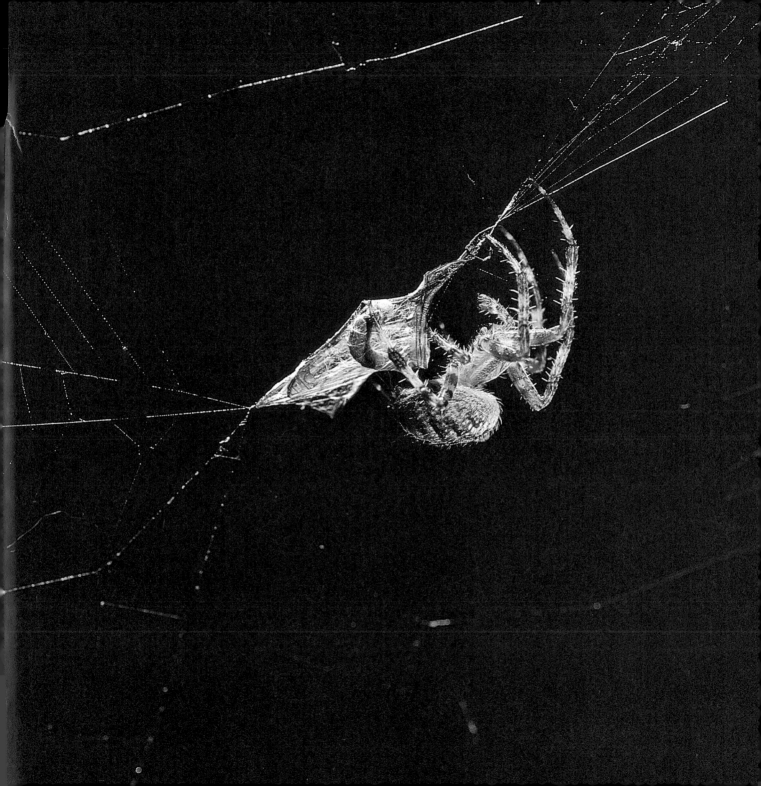

The spider eats the insect.

The spider is hungry. She carries the insect to the middle of the web. Then the spider begins to eat. She sucks all the juices out of the insect and leaves the hard outerskin behind.

When the spider has finished eating, she takes a rest.

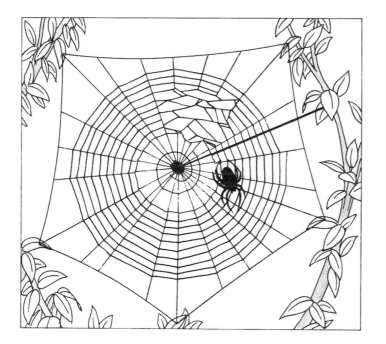

Later, she will start to make a new web.
Then what do you think will happen?

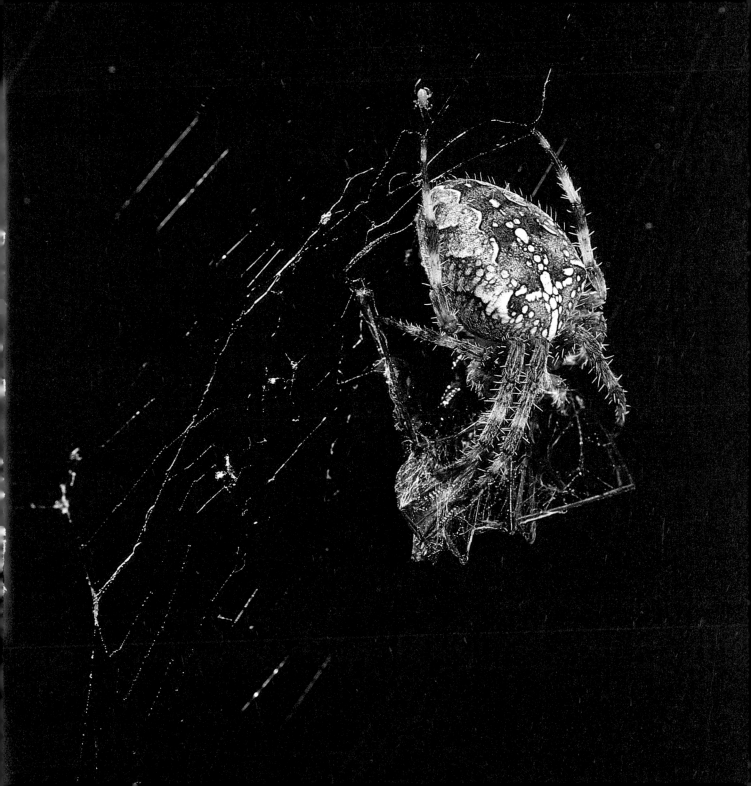

Do you remember how the spider makes her web?
See if you can tell the story in your own words.
You can use these pictures to help you.

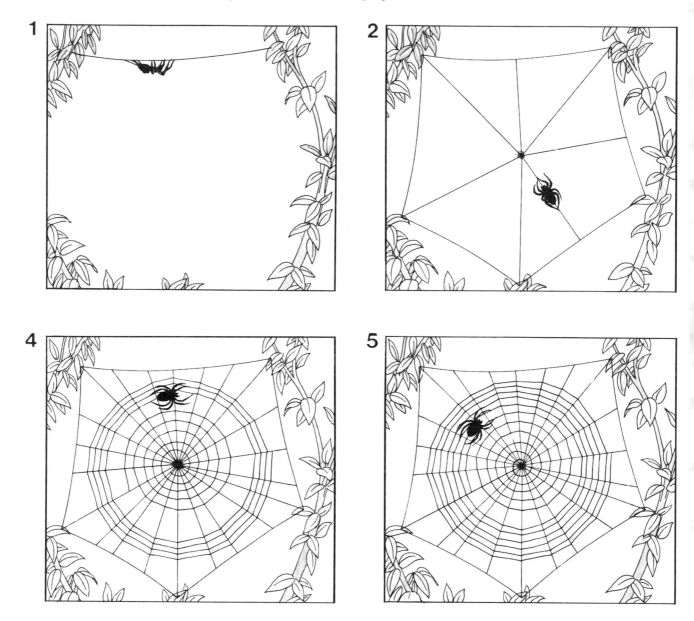

3

6

Index

This index will help you to find some of the important words in the book.

Now look out for spiders' webs in parks and gardens. You might see a spider building its web, or an insect caught in the web.